I0181892

GOING TO THE NEXT LEVEL

REVISED EDITION

GORDON MOORE

Ark House Press
PO Box 1722, Port Orchard, WA 98366 USA
PO Box 1321, Mona Vale NSW 1660 Australia
PO Box 318 334, West Harbour, Auckland 0661 New Zealand
arkhousepress.com

© 2015 Gordon Moore

All rights reserved. No part of this publication may be reproduced, stored in a retrieval system or transmitted in any form or by any means electronic, mechanical, photocopying, recording or otherwise without the prior written permission of the publisher.

Cataloguing in Publication Data:
Title: Going to the Next Level
ISBN: 9780994367563 (pbk.)
Subjects: Church growth/Leadership
Other Authors/Contributors: Moore, Gordon

Design and layout by initiateagency.com

Contents

I have personally known Gordon Moore for more than 30 years and have observed his leadership capacity and passion to inspire others to grow and progress in their lives and ministries, and therefore, I am confident to recommend his new book 'Going to the Next Level'.

This is a timely book that will empower pastors and churches to capture the initiative. It contains practical keys and advice that will enable pastors to progress to the next level of church life.

In his roles as the Australian National Director and a C3 Church Global Director, Gordon is well qualified as a mentor and coach of pastors to write his book for the local church practitioner. There is something to glean from this book for every senior minister, from planting a church to a mega church!

You're going to love it!

Phil Pringle
Founder & President
C3 Church Global

For years I have been puzzled, at times even frustrated, when I've seen pastors under my oversight seem to reach a ceiling or barrier in growing their churches and simply get stuck. These have been great people who were totally committed to Christ, were praying hard, working hard and loving the people under their care, but just couldn't seem to find their way into a positive, healthy, growing future. Some have simply given up concluding, "Pastoring a church is not for me!"

This experience set me on a quest to find a way to help these sincere and awesome pastors. After a long journey of prayer, research and trial and error, it finally dawned on me that its not the personality of the pastor, or the church, or the city, or the denomination that stops growth and progress in a church – it's the pastor's leadership style! This simple insight developed into my first book, **'Leadership Styles and Levels of Church'**, which has been instrumental in unlocking pastors and churches all over the world and propelling them into a positive and growing future.

It has been a privilege and honour to be able to share

these keys, first in my own movement of churches (C3 Church Global) and then in other denominations, and to see many pastors and churches literally revolutionised through the adoption and application of the leadership style principles I have identified.

This new book, **Going to the Next Level**, is a kind of postscript to the earlier work and is all about the outworking of the journey. It is written for the local church practitioner working at the coalface of daily church life. Each chapter outlines some key approaches and practices that can help pastors take their churches forward to a new level of growth.

I trust this book helps you to 'go to the next level!'

Gordon Moore Ph. D
Author

Chapter One

GETTING STARTED

GOING THROUGH THE 75 LEVEL

The first level of church growth (up to around 75 members) is called the 'Birth Level'. This is the formation stage of a church. Most churches begin with a small 'core group' that grows to a 'primary group' or around 50 to 75 members. This primary group typically consists of a pastor, several key supporters and influencers, and some members. Primary group churches make up 51 per cent of all churches, which means that half of all churches plateau at this level[1].

Right Seed Equals Right Tree

Everything in the kingdom of God begins with a seed. In fact, the kingdom of God is the kingdom of the seed (Matthew 13). It is important, therefore, that the founding pastor does not become focused on the numerical growth of the new church, but rather on the nature and quality of the seed being planted. It's not just how we begin that counts, it's how we finish!

When the Seed is Right, the Tree Will be Right!

This is a key foundational principle to how the kingdom of God works. A seed looks nothing like the tree, but it is what is hidden and located in the seed, that will determine both the visible outward form and the inward spiritual nature of the church in the future. That is the principle of the seed – when we get the seed right, the tree will be right! The Birth Level of a church is an important stage as this is when the foundations and directions of the new church are being established. The church's 'DNA' is being developed and modelled through the life of the founding pastor and begins to be articulated in the form of a vision. If a church is formed on the wrong foundations, or for the wrong motives or reasons, the seed will be faulty and as a result, the tree itself will be faulty as it grows and progresses into its future.

The Power of Culture

The formation of the culture of the church is vital. Culture is formed through the life, purpose and values of the founding leader. One of the common temptations for planting pastors can be to move too quickly for the sake of growth, placing people in roles and positions of influence who have not yet embraced his purpose, values and culture.

When new people are allowed to modify the culture, whether by default or intentionally, the purpose and values of the founding pastor will change – and vice versa. Therefore, much care and vigilance needs to be exercised in order to protect the purpose, values and culture of the newly planted church. These are the kernels of the seed. They are the heartbeat of the new church.

The Death of the Innocent

As illustrated in the lives of Moses and Jesus, one of the devil's key strategies has always been to strike the 'seed' (the infant) before it can become established. The founding pastor needs to be watchful for 'wolves', 'hirelings' and 'weird ones' that might destroy the seedling church. This is why more church planters today are adopting the practice of restricting the membership of a church planting team and developing an interview process to qualify any transferring members into the new church plant, rather than simply accepting anyone who turns up for the sake of numerical increase.

New Christians rarely have a problem with the culture of a church because they're born into it. It's Christians transferring from other churches and ministries who may come with issues, hurts, agendas, beliefs and practices that belong to another culture. Time must be given to the transitioning of transferring Christians into the church. This is true for any church at any level of growth.

The Permanency Factor

Establishing the permanency of a new church is a very important issue for the primary group church. This is about establishing the message that 'we are here to stay' and that 'you can trust us and depend on us'. A simple key to this is to live, work and socialise in your community. We now make it a requirement for planting pastors that they first move into their new community so they become seen and known. In short, they must become part of their new community.

Key Areas to Emphasise

Creating a High Relational Quotient

The pastor must initiate and facilitate relational opportunities through hospitality (get togethers, social and food occasions) both inside and outside the Sunday Services. In fact, we have adopted the approach that this should happen before the commencement of Sunday services. The planting of a church is all about the formation of a 'community of faith within a community', not the 'conducting of services to a community'.

Focusing on the Provision of Pastoral Ministry

At this level, the focus of ministry needs to be on effectively pastoring the members of the church, this is, preaching, teaching and ministering to the heartfelt needs of individuals. This is the primary responsibility and task of the pastors of the church, to be shared as the church grows.

Providing the Personal Contact of Every Member

At the Birth Level (as at any level of church growth) success is dependent upon what happens outside of the Sunday service. Visiting or personally contacting new people is vital so that the following things can happen:-

- The sowing of the pastor's purpose, values and heart
- Personal ministry to the heartfelt needs of the people by the pastor
- Identifying and encouraging any potential ministry and career directions of members
- Vigilant follow-up of all new people by the pastor so that they become established in the church
- The pastor is aware of any problems that arise and may move quickly to correct them

We have observed that too many pastors either delegate this task too quickly or never engage in effective pastoral care of the members in the first place. As a general rule, we require planting pastors to pastor every member personally until the church breaks through the 200+ level. The math is simple: 200 adult members divided by 40 weeks a year (allowing generously for 12 weeks holidays and other breaks) requires the pastor to connect personally and pastorally with only five members each week. If half of those members are married, then the number drops to 2-3 'pastoring moments' each week. Not a heavy workload by any stretch of the imagination.

Beginning to 'Share the Care' of the Members

Once membership reaches 75+, it is important to have already implemented a care program that has identified and included any emerging leaders. Avoid giving people positions and titles at this embryonic stage. Experience has found that it is more beneficial simply to encourage members to 'help the pastor' and to use language such as 'caring', 'sharing', and 'working together as a team'. The key idea here is to include others and share the load, rather than delegating and departmentalising (this will come later).

Keeping the 'Home Front' Healthy

We have observed over the years that many pastors try to go to a full-time salary with their church too quickly. The typical church at this level simply cannot support a full-time pastor without other areas of the church suffering from a lack of needed funds. We believe it to be sound advice to suggest that a pastor should phase in financial support from the church from around 75 members. Besides, contact with the unchurched through outside work can lead to conversions and valuable contacts in the community. It is far better to phase in financial support gradually from around 75 through to around 200 members. Furthermore, it is important that the pastor's family have financial stability.

Key Breakthrough Areas for 75 Level Church

There are key breakthrough areas at all levels of church

life. For the Birth Level church these can be summed up as follows:

- The pastor needs to build a core of new Christians and key members upon which to build the church. The best way to build a team is from new converts and those members who demonstrate a sense of ownership of the purpose, values and culture of the church.

- The pastor needs to continually sow the vision of the future of the church into a committed nucleus of emerging leaders and committed members.

- The pastor must begin to develop and involve others in assisting with ministry, this is, building a team based on strong relationships where all are involved in sharing the ministry of growing the church. The focus should not be on titles, positions and roles, but rather on working together with the pastor to 'make our church happen'.

Chapter Two

'GREAT POSSIBILITIES'
GOING THROUGH THE 100 LEVEL

Once a church has established itself and has broken through the 75+ level, the dynamics of the church begin to change. The church now feels like a 'going concern'. There is excitement in the air! Energy is no longer focused on 'getting started', but rather on starting to do things! That is why churches at this level, ranging from 75 through to 200 members, are called 'Possibility Churches'.

These churches have broken through the primary group zone of up to 75 members. Now most church events and activities are big enough to have impact and to allow visitors a sense of anonymity because they can blend into the crowd. Furthermore, there are now enough resources to make it possible to achieve more things and the formation of new church departments is a reality (oh, what a feeling!).

Creating a Sense of Atmosphere
One of the possibilities for the 100+ church is the ability to begin to create a sense of atmosphere in the

church, through the church's services, departments and activities. By and large, this is achieved through the music and the larger group dynamics that come with this size of church.

Mobilising the Church into Personal Evangelism

Modelling and creating a culture of relating to, including and influencing the unchurched and assimilating them into the church is a major key for growing a church.

Emphasising a departmental evangelism strategy is vital for the ongoing growth of a church. As the church grows, evangelism needs to be intentional, so early training and modelling on how to 'close the deal' with our friends is an important strategy; not just relating to our unchurched friends, but also learning how to influence them into making a commitment to Jesus Christ and the church.

This needs to become the standard operating procedure of all church departments, because as the church expands growth needs to happen through the departments, not just the pastor and the Sunday services.

Key Breakthrough Area for 100 Level Churches

For the Possibility Church, the key breakthrough areas can be summed up as follows:

-       The development of age/life stage activities and programs to ensure that your church is beginning to provide a growing inventory of service and programs to meet the diverse needs of new people and members

- The need to settle the facility issue to give the Possibility Church a seven-days-a-week presence and operational capacity and to further enhance a sense of permanency within the community

- The need for the church to reposition itself from being perceived as a 'small family church' to a 'growing, dynamic church' where there is 'room enough for everyone!'

- The breaking up of the primary group that was instrumental in getting things started. This is vital to the ongoing health and growth of the church. The reality is that what got you started will stop you growing! Failure to achieve this will, by default, create a dysfunctional church that will have:-

  o A tight, impenetrable 'in' group that wields all the power and influence

  o A 'cliquey' culture where newcomers feel unwelcome and are unable to form friendships

  o A 'fat cow' church where the members are consumers rather than contributors to a demanding vision and growing congregation

  o A leadership that rests in the hands of unfruitful members who tend to exercise

> influence on the basis of length of time served and proximity to the pastor - Fruitfulness is the paradigm of growing churches

Breaking up the primary group is achieved by inviting others, especially new converts and successful, fruitful transferring members, into positions and roles of influence in the church. Only those members of the primary group who are able to cope and grow with the new level and demands of the Possibility Church should be included as well.

This is the first big test of leadership for the pastor and the church. Experience reveals that pastors who are unable to lead their churches through this transition will stay at around the 75 to 150 level until change occurs.

- Vigilance in establishing proper administration and record-keeping systems and procedures. Minutes, timesheets, follow-up reports, pastoral and departmental contact reports and so on are all essential for the effective management of a growing membership. It is now impossible simply to rely only on memory!
- It is vital that the pastor require all appointed leaders to be directly accountable to him. During this time of growth and momentum, things can easily drift off course as the culture of the church is still being established.

- The pastor needs to develop in the church an awareness of church structure. As the church is expanding, it needs to 'get organised' in order to cope with and maintain the growth and momentum that is occurring. It is important, therefore, that the pastor work directly with all new leaders in establishing and building new departments and ministries in the Possibility Church.

Chapter Three

'FROM MINISTRY TO LEADERSHIP'
GOING THROUGH THE 200 LEVEL

Our personal experience and consultation with other churches has led us to the conclusion that breaking through the 200+ level is the most difficult transition to achieve and maintain. Statistics support this observation because around 86% of all churches are smaller than 200 members[2], with the average size of Pentecostal churches in Australia being around 131 members[3].

In the Australian church scene, we have identified four possible contributors to the 'less-than-200-member-church syndrome'. Our consultation with and observation of churches worldwide indicate that these factors apply universally, although in differing intensities.

1. There is a commonly held belief in Christian circles that **'small is better'**, although this way of thinking has been seriously challenged in recent years by the strong emergence of the so-called 'mega church', both here in the Australia and around the world.

2. In my first book on this subject, Leadership Styles and Levels of Church, I put forward the hypothesis that the style of leadership that is required to lead a large church is 'choleric-melancholic', but that this runs counter to the natural and prevailing 'sanguine-phlegmatic' personality that, according to the organisation MyCoach, makes up around 84 per cent of the nation of Australia.

3. A **'do-it-yourself'** mentality coupled with an emphasis on church planting at all costs can create a landscape in which there is much activity and impressive church planting statistics, but unimpressive church growth statistics. This situation tends to produce a plethora of small, non-viable churches that have not broken through the 75+ level, and probably never will.

4. It is our observation that churches traditionally tend to be planted **'pastorally'** and **'evangelistically'**. The emerging trend, however, is to plant churches **'apostolically'**, which gives the church plant a higher viability factor because of the resources and leadership input available from day one through an apostolic leader.

The Personal Contact Level (PCL)

One of the most obvious breakthrough characteristics at this level is the need for the pastor to begin to move away from having direct, personal and pastoral contact with every member of the church. This occurs through the delegation of the care of members to other pastors and leaders who emerge as associates to the senior pastor of the church. This process is very important to the future health and growth of the church. The pastor must move from 'ministry' to 'leadership'.

To sum up, then, the 'large church feeling' has arrived when:-

- Evangelism is beginning to happen naturally
- Departments begin to function in their own right
- The pastor is unable personally to cover the whole church effectively

Key Areas to Emphasise

Educating members about the 'Personal Contact Level'

For the 200+ church to continue growing, the pastor can no longer be personally available for the regular or primary care of church members. His role must now be to handle only 'critical care' situations, so that, increasingly, members are referred to the senior pastor by other leaders and pastors only when major matters arise.

Personally appointing, training, and mentoring key leaders

A monthly leaders' meeting is an ideal forum in which

to impart vision and basic pastoral and ministry skills to those to whom the care of members has been delegated. This is in addition to more frequent (e.g. bi-weekly) one-on-one meetings with each leader. The producing of a 'ministry manual' at this level can also be a positive tool to help bring focus in this area.

Key Breakthrough Areas for 200 Level Churches

For the church at the 200+ level, the key breakthrough areas can be summed up as follows:

- Appointment of assistant pastoral staff and lay pastors (positions need not necessarily be paid or full-time)
- Members understand that, of necessity, access to the senior pastor, who has made the shift from 'shepherd' to 'rancher', becomes more limited
- Establishing that the senior pastor's clear mandate and first priority is to lead and grow the church, assisted by his staff and a committed team of leaders
- Guarding against a small church mentality in attitude and practice (e.g. in-house chitchat, jokes and behaviour that can alienate new people from 'the club')

For the Pastor and Spouse

The pastor and spouse must begin to make themselves unavailable to every member (hence the PCL) as they move into the role of 'senior pastor', the 'pastor of the pastors' and 'leader of the leaders'. The pastor can no longer hope to have a hand in everything, but his 'voice' must be in everything. The pastor moves into the role of 'overseer' of the church. As such, his function is that of:-

- The vision caster
- The voice of authority to the church
- The agent of raising up, releasing and empowering ministers and leaders in the church
- The leader of a team of leaders
- The chairperson of the board

There needs to be a stronger sense of leaders being accountable by shifting to a 'results and fruitfulness' paradigm. All ministry accountability needs to be through an established system of formal reporting; otherwise it will be impossible to know what is going on in the church.

The 200+ church runs on a 'vision, values and policy' basis rather than a 'personal' basis. That is to say that, because the church can no longer be covered effectively just by the personality and force of one pastor, policies need to be established that reflect the purpose, values and culture of the church, irrespective of which individuals are involved in delivering ministry or leadership.

It is also vital to establish and maintain a 'spirit of excellence' in every area, department and ministry of the church. As leadership and ministry are delegated more and more, standards and expectations can tend to become diminished, thus reducing the effectiveness of the church and its ministry.

For Leaders

Leaders need to expand and grow personally to be able to cope with the bigger scenario and environment of a larger church. They need to rise to a higher level of spiritual maturity.

Leaders should not all expect to have direct access to the senior pastor. All leaders must accept that they might not be informed of or involved in every decision and program. A higher level of trust is required.

All leaders need to become strong carriers of the vision of the church. When asked about the church's vision, the leader's immediate response is, "This is our vision, direction, policy and way of doing things," not, "You'll have to ask Pastor – I don't know." **Every leader must know the vision!**

Leaders in 200+ churches must develop a higher level of submission and accountability to the senior pastor. This will create an atmosphere of honour and accountability throughout the entire church. That means there are no personal agendas or directions or approaches to leadership. Every leader is totally into the senior pastor's direction for the church (we commonly refer to this as 'buy-in'). One of the reasons churches don't grow is when everyone is simply doing their own thing so that the efforts of the church are fragmented and there is no sense of team.

For Members

Members of 200+ churches need to embrace the idea that they are no longer in a small church. They need to embrace:-

- Bigger ideas
- Bigger dimensions
- Bigger departments and ministries
- Bigger money
- Bigger crowds
- Etc.…

They must accept the fact that, although they still identify the senior pastors as their pastors, they will not be pastored by them personally. One way to help this process is to change the title of 'Senior Pastor' to 'Senior Minister' once the church grows through 200 members and other pastors are doing the actual pastoring.

Members need to rise to the challenge of accepting that this will cost more money, as more staff are needed to run the church and to pastor the people.

They must also accept that they will only be involved in and familiar with a portion of what is happening in the church. In other words, they won't know all about everything that is going on.

At this level, the church has moved on from 'the old days' when:-
-     'We were all known'
-     'We were all involved'
-     'We were all informed
-     'We were all influencers'

Our church used to small enough for all ages to mix together: we were one happy family! Now the church is one big, extended, happy family!

Chapter Four

'THE COMFORT ZONE'
GOING THROUGH THE 500 LEVEL

The 500+ level is commonly referred to as the 'Comfort Zone' because a church at this level can do most things well without having to struggle for resources or people. Almost 98% of all churches are smaller than 500 members[4]! In the church scene, 500+ churches are also often called 'credibility level churches' simply because of their size, resources and influence.

The most obvious characteristic of a 500+ church is that it is now large enough to do most things on its own. It no longer needs to participate in 'unity events', most of which are initiated by small churches that are wanting to make a bigger impact but are unable to do so by themselves.

The reason for this extra capacity is that 500+ churches have multiple ministries and departments that cater for all ages and life stages. In short, specialisation of functions and ministries occurs at every level in the 500+ church. Furthermore, 500+ churches are able to expand locally, regionally and internationally more effectively through church planting and missions programs.

Unique 500+ 'Problems'

This level of church presents its own set of problems and challenges that must be negotiated and solved by the senior minister. The first of these is **managing the business of the church**. With a church of this size, there is now something happening somewhere at all times! Many pastors experience burnout at this stage as they try to balance the demands of a large church with family commitments and the increasing number of opportunities to influence and impact beyond their own church that comes with proven fruitfulness and experience.

The most important questions to ask are:-

- "What am I called to do?"
- "Am I called to lead this church or to itinerate?"
- "Can I grow this church if I'm not here?"
- "What activities are detrimental to our growth and health?"

In other words, the senior minister must focus on the task at hand and set his priorities accordingly, or suffer the consequences! The old maxim holds true, 'you can't have your cake and eat it too!'

The Comfort Zone can become a permanent state if the senior minister loses focus on what his real priorities are. It takes a lot of energy, skill and commitment to be effective as the senior minister of a large, growing and influential 500+ church.

The second problem to be negotiated is the **administration of the 'stuff'** that accumulates as a result of the business of a 500+ church. So much so in fact that some commentators over the years have referred to this level of church as the 'administration level'. How true this is!

In my first book, I described this level as the 'Choleric Level', that is, the level of the strategic, organised, managed and facilitated church. Leaders who cannot, or will not, make the shift to becoming strategic in their leadership style will simply fail to lead their churches into the 500+ zone and beyond. It's basically a matter of 'get organised or stagnate!' It is essential therefore, that the senior minister gives special attention to the administration of the church to avoid the danger of costly duplications and mistakes. The delegation of responsibility for every department and ministry to associates who are directly accountable to the senior minister is vital.

A third area of importance is the priority of **keeping very close to your key leaders**. Business and the demands of the large church can undermine the most important aspect of church life: relationships. There is simply no room for error or neglect in this area.

All large churches that are healthy and growing have strong leadership teams of people who have long-term relationships and are committed to each other. They are not just doing a job, they are deeply committed to each other and actually love what they're doing together.

The fourth problem for 500+ churches is the **danger of dilution and fractioning** of the organisation. This can occur in any large organisation where a department is able to exist in and of itself, rather than as part of the whole. It is vital therefore, that every leader, department and ministry in the church be held accountable to the purpose, values and culture of the whole church. There must be a tangible and assessable measuring stick for this accountability that measures each department's contribution to the overall purpose and goals of the church.

We call this process/system of accountability 'templating'. It is established through effective communication with and between every church department, ministry and program, so that all roles, expectations and desired results are clarified before any activity occurs. Afterwards follow-up, debrief and a critiquing process are used to measure outcomes. In short, communication is king!

A fifth challenge for the senior minister of the 500+ church is to **transition major departments** into

200+ congregations in their own right. This is a vital process as it sets the 500+ church up to become a 1000+ church, where growth results from each department/region contributing to the health and growth of the church as a whole.

Key Breakthrough Areas for the 500 Level Church

For the Comfort Zone church, the key breakthrough areas can be summed up as follows:

- The need to streamline the roles of the senior minister and other staff, as well as those of the board and ministry leaders.

- The potential problem of the dilution of the church's purpose and core values through over-involvement in 'extracurricular' activities. That is, through seemingly worthwhile involvements that detracts from the fulfilment of the purpose, vitality and growth of the church.

- The development of effective 'high visibility events' and celebration services to draw new people.

- The introduction of congregational, mid-sized activities and events for groups of less than 200 becomes very important. For example, demographic 'regions' such as adults, youth, men, women, business people and children all need a setting in which cater for the specific needs of those members and new people being reached.

- An effective pastoral system must be in place. Defining and delegating pastoral care along the lines of 'primary care' (done by small group leaders) versus 'critical care' (done by the pastors of the church) is a great strategy that has served us well.

- The raising up and placement of 200+ level leaders over every department.

Observations and Conclusions about 500+ Churches

Our experience and observations have led us to the following conclusions about 500+ level churches:

- The 500+ church is unlike 98 per cent of all churches! What works in a 75+ level church or a 200+ level church, for example, does not work in a 500+ level church.

- Many pastors do not understand that 500+ churches are different. They believe that if they faithfully just keep doing what they've been doing, then somehow God will give them continued growth. The reality, however, is this: every leader continually needs to change and adapt to new ways of leading in order to be effective at the next level of church growth.

From feedback and discussions with pastors of smaller churches, we have found that these pastors tend to identify the following reasons for why some churches grow to 500+ while theirs hasn't.

- The areas in which 500+ churches are located make it easier to grow a church
- 500+ pastors are naturally better leaders
- Some just put it down to what I call 'Christian luck', that is, they just happen to be in the right place at the right time and growth just happens!

Contrary to these beliefs, however, we have consistently found that most 500+ pastors are not necessarily better leaders. The are simply doing the things that lead to consistent growth over long periods of time and, in the process, have become great leaders, irrespective of their location or denomination!

A significant recent development in Australia has been the 500+ conferences, initiated and convened by Phil Baker, Senior Minister of Riverview Church in Perth. These conferences bring together pastors of 500+ level churches from all denominations for the purposes of networking, idea exchange and input. Phil Baker has made the comment a number of times that the power of these conferences is in the fact that the 500+ church is unlike other churches, irrespective of denomination or style, and that senior ministers of 500+ churches have a lot in common[5].

Our conclusion goes a step further. We would argue that this principle applies to all levels of church. The generic approach so often adopted in Bible colleges and at conferences and other leadership training forums is proving to be ineffective precisely because of these differences. We have found that it is more productive to teach leadership specifically to the level at which that leader will be leading. For example, the leadership style and skills required to plant a church are totally different to the leadership style and skills required to lead a 500+ church. A whole new skill set is required to lead such a church. We have found that the secret to constantly going to the next level is always to be learning how to lead at the next level.

Chapter Five

'THE MEGA CHURCH'
GOING THROUGH THE 1000 LEVEL

The Rise of the Mega Church

Though they currently account for only three-tenths of one per cent of all churches, recent research by the Hartford Institute for Religion Research in the United States reveals that mega churches are on the rise and showing strong growth rates[6].

According to the Hartford Institute's "Mega Churches Today 2005" research report, common characteristics of mega churches "such as adaptation to change, sense of being spiritually vital, having a clear mission as well as youthfulness of the congregation and the use of guitars and drums, and the rates at which members tell others about the church are significant variables in terms of growth and health of the churches[7]".

Building the Senior Team

Churches that grow through the 1000 level and beyond have typically developed senior leadership teams of close knit and specialised leaders who are all contributing to the growth and development of the church. A

1000+ church simply cannot be led, coordinated and pastored by one person. Therefore, highly qualified and productive teams emerge in the mega church.

Such churches have eliminated all traces of small church mentality from their thinking and practice. Churches of 1000+ are referred to as 'mega churches' because of their size, momentum, resources and influence.

Mega Churches can 'Get Stuck'

All churches at any level can 'get stuck', that is, they can plateau or 'flat-line' in their spiritual health, vitality, progress and growth. For the mega church in particular, such a loss of momentum can be very difficult to regain. It takes a much greater effort to turn around a large ocean going vessel that it does a small dinghy. Momentum, therefore, is sacred and must never be compromised.

There are several factors that can cause a loss of momentum. The most common and perilous for the mega church is simply loss of focus. The larger the church, the greater the danger of distraction and being diverted from the core purpose and values that established and grew the church in the first place.

A second cause of mega churches becoming stuck is a breakdown in relationships among the senior team. In smaller churches, relationships breakdown often occurs between members and the pastor. In the mega church, however, there are more people working together at high levels of activity and influence. It is essential, therefore, that much time and effort be given by all parties to ensure that these important relationships are maintained in a healthy state.

The 'Presidential Level'

We describe this level of church as the 'Presidential Level' because of the nature and style of leadership in churches that break through the 1000+ level. A more presidential style of leadership ensures that the mega church keeps progressing and growing.

It is important not only that the senior leader understand this concept of 'presidential leadership', but also the rest of the senior leadership team who must work together as a 'presidential team' in leading a church of this size. In churches of less than 1000, the purpose and values of the church are worked out directly through the senior leader's involvement and activity. But in the 1000+ church, this process happens indirectly through the senior team, rather than directly through the senior leader. It is the capacity of a senior leader to develop a team of gifted, strong, influential and fruitful leaders that creates and grows the mega church.

The term 'presidential' refers to the way senior leaders need to act and deport themselves and exercise their leadership within the mega church setting. The following is a brief description of this style of leadership.

Headship

The senior leader must accept the reality that he is now the 'head' of the church rather than the 'minister' or 'pastor' of the church. This might sound like mere semantics, but it is actually important to make this distinction. His responsibility is prayerfully to assume leadership with confidence and competence and in so doing to release others to manage, minister to and pastor the church. His role is to provide leadership at a macro level. He must not for any reason get involved in micro leadership of the church organisation. If he does the church will begin to falter and lose momentum.

To Preside

According to the Microsoft Thesaurus, 'to preside' means:-

- To take the chair
- To control
- To supervise
- To be in charge of
- To direct
- To officiate
- To keep order

Presiding is the equivalent of the scriptural idea of 'overseeing', that is, to be set in a place or position of watching over the church. The crucial role of the senior leader of the mega church is prayerfully and intuitively to see what needs to be done and to exert all necessary influence, authority and control to bring direction, order, health and fruitfulness to the church.

Statesman-like

One of the greatest needs in the mega church is for the constant, clear articulation of its purpose, values and direction. High-level communication skills are not just an added bonus or a nice-to-have, they are an indispensable element of the skill set of the senior leader and senior team members. All members of the senior leadership team must be presidential in their communication style: all communicating one drumbeat to the church with one voice and one heart.

To communicate direction or instructions in an unclear of confused manner is to set sail with power, influence and momentum but without a rudder. Disaster awaits on a mega scale!

Commander-in-Chief

The senior leader of the mega church must 'lead the charge' by providing great exemplary leadership that sets the right spiritual tone, rallies the troops and keeps the ship on course towards its all-important purpose.

Both the senior leader and the senior team must recognise that the initiative and responsibility for making important and difficult decisions rests with them, especially in the heat of battle. There can be no indecision. There can be no 'delegating upwards'. The senior leader, assisted by the senior team, has assumed command and is leading strong.

The Appointment of 'Entrepreneurial Leaders'

The senior leadership team and heads of departments in the mega church must be effective directors of other people and resources, not just 'doers' or hands-on leaders. In their book, 'The Boardroom Entrepreneur', Southon and West are very helpful in explaining the critical need for entrepreneurial leaders **within** any progressive organisation. This is consistent with the biblical presentation of the kingdom of God as an entrepreneurial kingdom. The kingdom of God is an advancing, progressive, taking-ground, increasing kingdom (Isaiah 9:6-7, Matt 11:2 TLB). Furthermore, the kingdom of God is portrayed in the Scriptures as the 'kingdom of the seed' (Mark 4:30-32), a metaphor that reflects the essential 'growth' nature of God's kingdom.

This entrepreneurial nature, the quintessential nature of the kingdom of God, is a ground-breaking, pioneering spirit producing kingdom leadership that is all about growing things from the seed of vision into a tangible harvest. This is especially true of the leadership gift of 'apostle', which, at its core, is the entrepreneurial spirit that expands the kingdom of God through initiating, pioneering, launching, birthing and creating. The original Greek word used in 1 Corinthians 12:28

to describe the order of importance of this gift and office in the church is 'proton', meaning 'first, at the beginning, chief'. It's from this word that we derive the English work, 'prototype'.

Ten Characteristics of Entrepreneurs

Southon & West offer the following list of entrepreneurial qualities[8]:

1. Entrepreneurs look beyond how things are to how they might be different.

2. Entrepreneurs have powerful idiosyncratic visions (that is, visions that are 'peculiar to an individual')

3. Entrepreneurs make things happen: they are people of action, not just visionaries.

4. Entrepreneurs possess the trait of determination. They will not take 'no' for an answer!

5. Entrepreneurs are ambitious, not to make money, but to change things.

6. Entrepreneurs are charismatic, "they attract followers; they get these people to jump through hoops. Business is a team game: if you cannot inspire and motivate people, you will not turn your idea into a working commercial entity."

1. Entrepreneurs are positive: "Their optimism is often delightfully irrational, but it needs to be."

2. Entrepreneurs are often in a great hurry: "They want things done yesterday. They are not always very tolerant of people who prefer to move more slowly."

3. Entrepreneurs are hard workers: "This may seem obvious but it's a key difference between people who sound like entrepreneurs – have lots of great ideas and can attract followers – and people who actually end up creating successful businesses."

4. Entrepreneurs choose to work in an environment with stratospherically high levels of uncertainty: "Entrepreneurs are not gamblers, that is, addicted to risk. The best entrepreneurs work hard to minimise risk once they have chosen their path."

The need to appoint 'Intrapreneurial leaders in 1000+ churches

It is essential to the ongoing health and growth of the mega church that all leaders embrace the 'entrepreneurial spirit' within their departments or ministries or areas of influence. Hence, the term, 'intrapreneurial'.

Departments must be seen as large networks, rather than small groups, within the church. One of the common and essential transitions that churches that break through the 1000+ level make is the development of large departmental networks within the church based on age/life-stage/lifestyle groupings. For example: adults, men, women, young families, single adults, youth, children, women and business people.

These departments must each become 'mega' (large) in their philosophy and approach to leadership. Departmental leaders can no longer run their departments as 'ministry groups', whereby the department leader ministers to a particular group of members. Just like leaders of 200+ level churches, they too must transition from being a minister to being a leader in their department by delegating all ministry activity to other leaders so that they can become the senior, visionary leader of that network. For example, churches that continue with a 'youth group' approach to youth ministry will never be able to grow the youth department beyond 100 to 200 young people.

What's critical about this is that such a department will no longer be contributing to the growth and development of the overall church, but rather will become a stagnant group within the church. But when each department is functioning as a healthy network, the mega church has the potential for unlimited growth because strategic leadership is functioning in every part of the church, not just at the senior leadership level. This is the nature of the 1000+ church: to have within itself the resources and momentum to be able to provide effective leadership at every level of church life.

Mega Churches Don't Need Mega Buildings

One of the common myths about mega churches is that they all have mega buildings. Recent research, however, shows this is simply not the case. According to the Hartford Institute for Religion Research, the average auditorium seating capacity for mega churches is 1400[9]. The conclusion? Mega churches maximise their facility usage by conducting multiple services on and off site.

A 'Mentoring Culture'

Because of the constant and high demand for a pool of new and rising leaders, intentional mentoring and training of leaders occurs at every level in the mega church. A potential danger for the mega church is to succumb to a pressing need for leaders and to short-circuit the mentoring process by 'hiring from without'. This may provide a short-term quick fix, but if the process is not managed well it can result in big problems. A mentoring culture will take longer to develop, but it results in a steady stream of leaders rising from within the church: 'sons and daughters of the house'.

An 'Engendering Culture'

'Serving as examples' (1 Peter 5:3) is a necessary characteristic of leadership in churches at all levels, but it is especially vital in Presidential Level churches.

The importance of creating a culture to carry church life so that it is consistent with the purpose and values of the church cannot be underestimated. The culture we believe in and aspire towards is the culture that we personally live by nature. Culture is not legislated. It is intrinsic to who we are and our core beliefs and how we view ourselves in the world. Culture, therefore, is developed over time and cannot be lived outside of who we really are.

This is why importing leaders into churches without a pathway that provides a process for them to adopt the church's culture poses a problem. Time and care must be taken for transitioning new leaders not just into understanding the culture, but into becoming part of the culture of the house.

We cannot demand conformity to culture of ourselves or others. It is about the kind of people we are and what we experience and share with others of like mind and spirit. For example, you cannot demand excellence from someone who doesn't really believe in the excellence of the House of God! They might conform for a season, but eventually what is in their heart will be obvious, for good or bad: *"for as he thinks in his heart, so is he; eat and drink, he says to you, but his heart is not with you." (Proverbs 23:7)*

Adopting the 'As If' Principle

The senior leaders of growing mega churches all convey the same spirit and approach when it comes to people, policies and procedures in the church. It's 'as if' the senior leader were there in person. There is a high level of unity and *esprit de corps*. It doesn't matter which leader is functioning because all are committed to the same purpose, values and attitude. In the mega church a dilution of excellence can occur outwards and downwards through the multiple layers of the church if all the senior leaders are not ensuring that consistent levels of excellence are being maintained throughout their spheres of responsibility and influence.

The 'Filter' Versus 'Sponge' Principle

The senior leader must build into the team of senior leaders an understanding that they need to be 'filters' rather than 'sponges' as they exercise leadership in the mega church. Sponges soak up and then dump when squeezed or placed under pressure. This is the dynamic of a leader who simply soaks up every complaint, attitude and negative report from others and then dumps indiscriminately on the senior leader and others when they've reached maximum capacity or are placed under pressure. In reality, this kind of leader is not exercising leadership at all, but is simply responding to and being influenced by others.

Filters, on the other hand, block out unwanted material. They discriminate and choose between substances and thus keep the system clean. This is the dynamic of a leader who blocks out and processes unnecessary and unwarranted complaints, attitudes and negative reports from others. He shares in an appropriate manner and at an appropriate time and place any helpful and constructive criticism or feedback that might help the senior leadership team be properly informed to lead more effectively and to maintain order in the church. This kind of leader is exercising leadership at a high level because he is not responding to or being influenced by others in a negative way at all. He is providing advocacy for the senior leaders and the church by exercising godly discrimination against attitudes and influences that pull down rather than build up the leaders and the church.

"But in a great house there are not only vessels of gold and of silver, but also of wood and of earth; and some to honour, and some to dishonour. Therefore if anyone purges himself from these, he shall be a vessel to honour, sanctified and useful to the Master, prepared for every good work." (2 Timothy 2:20-21)

Understanding and Valuing What God Has Given You

Churches that have reached the 1000+ level have had to come to a clear understanding of the distinctives that God has given them. A church at this level has successfully transitioned through the phase of trying to figure out what God wants them to be and do, they now know this. One of the things that restricts the growth and development of churches, especially 1000+ churches, is the trap of copying other church models, systems and programs. This can lead to a faddish culture that is always looking for the latest program or system from outside that will bring growth. Growth comes from the inner health of the church community, not from without. Christian Schwarz, founder of the Natural Church Development approach to church growth calls this the 'all by itself' factor or the '65 Hypothesis'. Specifically, his research has shown that when a church has eight essential health characteristics in high measure, the church will grow 'all by itself'[10].

Learning from other leaders and churches is important and all great leaders do this. But the real skill a leader needs to develop is the ability to identify and apply principles, not just models or programs, within his particular setting. Copying a program is a common mistake of leaders who have not yet developed a clear sense of their own individuality and the uniqueness of the calling and purpose that God has given to them and their church. This idea is clearly illustrated by the fact that Jesus did not send one common letter to the apostles of the seven churches in the book of Revelation. One the contrary, each apostle and church was send a specific detailed letter from the Spirit about their particular situation.

"To the angel of the church of Ephesus write... he who has an ear, let him hear what the Spirit says to the churches." (Revelation 2:1,7)

The 'Apostolic Centre'

I believe that the calling and responsibility of every mega church is to be a resource centre for the Kingdom of God. This is confirmed by the observation that most Senior Ministers of mega churches, for example, are involved in much wider worlds than their own individual churches.

Their lives are busy about setting standards and examples of innovation and leadership through their own churches, initiating church planting and missions world wide, developing networks for the mentoring and coaching of pastors and leaders, accepting leadership and oversight roles in denominations which primarily care for smaller churches, and exercising godly influence into their communities and nations.

We are living in an incredible season of God-given favour where the Body of Christ is seeing a massive increase in the number of these 'apostolic centres'. This will mean the release of tens of thousands of apostles from these centres, backed and resourced by their growing and healthy mega churches, who will make a significant impact on the unchurched world. Bring on this apostolic season!

FAQs

Over recent years we have been privileged to share this model at many pastors and leaders conferences, as well as in other forums and training settings. We have kept a record of questions that have been frequently asked. Here are our answers to some of those questions:

"How do we become or make ourselves bigger people?"

The starting point is to admit that we need to grow and become bigger people. This takes humility and a willingness to learn from others. One of the best ways to become a bigger person is to associate with bigger people. If I surround myself with small-thinking leaders, I will be locked into the same level of thinking. Bigger people challenge me; they provoke me to grow; the way they think and live pushes me beyond my comfort zones. We all need this, no matter what level we are at.

I have made it a practice regularly to seek out opportunities to mix with bigger leaders than myself. I have found that if I ask, most are willing to give the time to answer my questions.

"Your model presents the concept of moving from one quadrant to another in an upward sense. What advice would you give to a pastors who has moved from a higher to a lower quadrant?"

First, such a pastor and his church need help – urgently! This can be a very painful and difficult time for a pastor and a congregation. Of course, the best scenario is to get help before this happens, but this is not always practical or available. The most important thing is to be honest, humble and open and to establish 'why' things have gone backwards. Identifying the truth, the whole truth, and nothing but the truth is the starting point. Once this is clear, the correct steps can be put in place to regain momentum.

Tip: This process needs to be in consultation with and guided by a pastor who has actually taken his church to the next level beyond yours.

"What would your advice be to a pastor who has tried everything and still cannot grow his church?"

My advice for a pastor in this demoralising situation would be to resign with dignity and to move on and find something at which he can be fruitful and successful.

Being the pastor of a church is not the sum total of life or the kingdom of God! I believe that God wants us to "prosper and be in health even as [our] souls prosper" (3 John 3). Therefore, prosperity and success in life are generally signs that we're probably in the right place. We have helped many pastors find their way into a more fruitful and productive life, some in other areas of ministry and others in secular fields. The key thing here is the 'viability' of the church. A church that is not growing and that has no sense of progress or future prospects is not viable, for the congregation or for the pastor and his family. My personal opinion is that a church doesn't begin to have viability until it reaches the 200+ level.

"What advice would you give to a pastor who has a 'big church mindset' and who is about to take over a church where the members have a predominantly 'small church mindset'?"
First, be sure that you have been called to take this on! Usually a mindset is just what it says – a 'set' mind!

You would need to know for how long this mindset has been part of the church culture and how strong it is. Before taking the church on, I would seek a commitment from all key leaders and influencers that they be prepared to resign from all positions and be prepared to change and follow you, not matter what the cost.

"How often do you cast the vision to your church?"

Every day, week, month and year! In other words, I cast vision in every situation and at every opportunity: in my attitude, conversation, preaching, teaching, advertising – everything! There is nothing more important than vision casting. Everything else in church life flows from the vision. Anything that doesn't needs to be excluded!

"Do you change your vision annually?"

We never change our vision! It is our raison d'être! The vision is the 'God purpose' that defines who you are and what you have been appointed by God to do. Goals change, strategies change, language changes, programs change, personnel change, but vision never changes! Vision is the ever-present constant. It is like the North Star in the sky: it provides our true north. It is the voice of God to the church guiding us to our bright future.

"What is the role and importance of boards in churches?"

This is a very important question, but needs to be answered according to the level of church.

First, the role of a board in the local church is to support, complement and partner with the senior minister to ensure the ongoing health and growth of the church and its ministries. The board fulfills this role by ensuring that the senior minister is provided with adequate and appropriate resources for achieving the church's purpose by working with the senior minister towards the successful achievement of the church's ends.

Second, boards are important because as the church grows spiritually and numerically it also grows materially in terms of finances, resources and property. So for the sake of prudence in matters of law, taxation and accountability, the senior minister appoints a board to partner with him and to act as trustees of the church's resources and property on behalf of Christ (the owner) and the church's members (the stakeholders).

Tip: A copy of an article entitled 'How to Run an Effective Board' by Dr Gordon Moore can be ordered by emailing enquiries@c3bd.com

"When should a church establish its own board?"

It has become standard practice for us not to establish a board in a new church plant. The sending church can provide this function for the new church. We establish a formal board once a church breaks through the 200+ level. The three main reasons for this policy are:

- Unnecessary resources, time and energy can be consumed in maintaining this structure for new and smaller churches;
- Leadership and financial accountability are very important in the formative stages of a new church plant; and,

- Time needs to be taken to choose the right people for the positions of board members.

"From your research and observation, what actually grows a church?"

This is an important question. The answer might not sound right when we first hear it because we are so influenced and driven by a prevailing ministry-oriented church culture.

Here's the answer: **Leadership grows the church!**

Let me explain. Ministry, that is, preaching, teaching, worship, prayer, visitation, prophecy, evangelism, etc., does not grow the church. All these things are essential to building and encouraging believers, but they do not grow the church. Most churches have all these 'ministry activities' happening, often at very proficient levels, and yet most churches are not growing! It is our observation that most churches have proficient ministers 'leading' the church, but that those 'leaders' are delivering 'ministry' not 'leadership'.

Leadership is the delivery of strategic goals and planning. It is about holding other leaders and ministers and activities accountable for results and placing leaders over the ministers throughout the whole congregation.

Bibliography

[1] Carl F. George, How to Break Growth Barriers, pp. 130-131

[2] National Church Life Survey, 2001

[3] For information regarding the 500+ conferences, contact: luisap@riverviewchurch.com.au

[4] Pauline J. Change, "Researchers Launch Extensive Survey on U.S. Mega Churches" The Christian Post, 27 July 2005 (www.christianpost.com)

[5] Scott Thumma, Dave Travis & Warren Bird, "Mega churches Today 2005: Summary of Research Findings", http://hirr.hartsem.edu/default.html

[6] Mike Southon & Chris West, The Boardroom

Entrepreneur, Random House, 2005, pp.13-17.

[7]Christian A. Schwarz, Natural Church Development, Churchsmart Resources, 1996, pp. 40-42.